THE ESSENTIAL COMPENDIUM OF

DAD JOKES

The Best of the Worst
Dad Jokes for the
Painfully Punny Parent

THE ESSENTIAL COMPENDIUM OF

DAD JOKES

The Best of the Worst
Dad Jokes for the
Painfully Punny Parent

EDITED BY THOMAS NOWAK
ILLUSTRATIONS BY KARL WHITELEY

CHRONICLE BOOKS
SAN FRANCISCO

Library of Congress Cataloging-in-Publication Data:
Names: Nowak, Thomas, editor.
Title: The essential compendium of dad jokes : the best of the worst
    dad jokes for the painfully punny parent / edited by Thomas Nowak.
Description: San Francisco : Chronicle Books, [2020].
Identifiers: LCCN 2019048982 | ISBN 9781452182797 (hardback)
Subjects: LCSH: Fathers—Humor. | Fatherhood—Humor. | American wit
    and humor. | BISAC: HUMOR / Form / Jokes & Riddles
Classification: LCC PN6231.F37 E87 2020 | DDC 818/.602—dc23
LC record available at https://lccn.loc.gov/2019048982

Manufactured in China.

Illustrations by Karl Whiteley.
Design by Jon Glick.

10 9 8 7 6 5 4

Chronicle Books LLC.
680 Second Street
San Francisco, CA 94107

www.chroniclebooks.com

CONTENTS

FOR DADDY, AKA HUDSON,
WHO ALWAYS HAS A CORNY JOKE
UP HIS SLEEVE

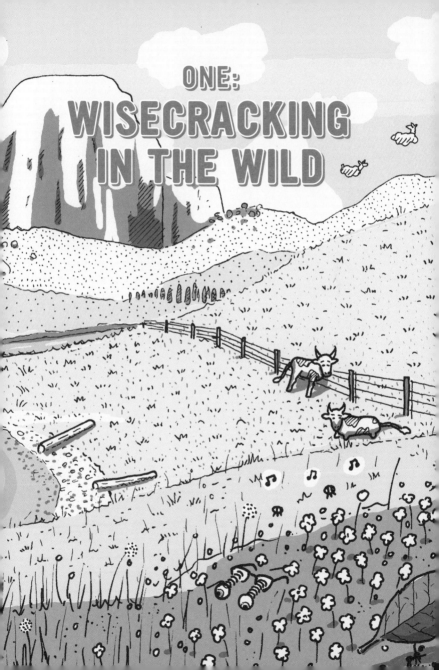

In my career
as a lumberjack,
I've cut exactly
2,324 trees.

If you ever encounter
a **GIANT**,

make sure to use big words.

Why is it always **COLD**
in stadiums?

Because they're full of fans!

My wife saw an
ANT pick up a **LEAF**
five times its
weight and said,
"Can you imagine being
that strong?"

So
I picked up
the leaf
and said,
"Yes."

What do you call a cow with **TWO** legs?

Lean beef.

If the cow has **NO** legs,

then it's ground beef.

How many tickles does it take to make an **OCTOPUS** laugh?

Ten–tickles.

You know what the **LOUDEST** pet you can get is?

A trumpet.

What do you get when you cross a **SNOWMAN** with a **VAMPIRE?**

Frostbite.

What do you call a sheep with NO LEGS?

A cloud.

What did the **BUFFALO** say to his **SON** when he dropped him off at school?

"Bison."

Why did the **SCARECROW** win an award?

Because he was out standing in his field!

I remember when
the **SHOVEL**
was invented.

It was truly a groundbreaking creation.

Two **GOLDFISH** are
in a **TANK**. One says
to the other,

"Do you know how to drive this thing?"

Why can you never find elephants when they hide in trees?

Because they're so good at it.

What do you call a dog that can do **MAGIC**?

A Labracadabrador.

What do you call an alligator in a **VEST**?

An investigator!

I used to have a job **COLLECTING LEAVES.**

I was raking it in.

What happens if a **FROG** parks illegally?

They get toad.

Why do **CRABS** never give to charity?

Because they're shellfish creatures!

Why couldn't you hear the **PTERODACTYL** go to the bathroom?

Because the P is silent!

Why do bees **HUM**?

???

Because they don't know the words!

I named my dogs **ROLEX** and **TIMEX**.

They're my watch dogs!

What's the difference between a **HIPPO** and a **ZIPPO**?

One's really heavy while the other one is a little lighter.

Did you hear about the **CIRCUS** fire?

It was in tents!

What do you call a pony with a **SORE THROAT**?

A little hoarse.

I just watched a program
about **BEAVERS**.

It was the best dam program
I've ever seen.

What did the **PIRATE** say on his **80**th birthday?

"Aye, matey!"

How can you tell if an **ANT** is a boy or a girl?

They're all girls, otherwise they'd be uncles.

How do you organize an **OUTER SPACE** party?

You planet.

I don't know why **TREES** make me so nervous . . .

I guess because they're so shady.

What type of magazines do **COWS** enjoy reading?

Cattlelogs.

What did the **OCEAN** say to the sailboat?

Nothing; it just waved.

What do you call an **ELEPHANT** that doesn't matter?

An irrelephant.

What did the mermaid wear to **MATH CLASS**?

An algae-bra.

What do you call a fish with **NO EYES?**

A fsh.

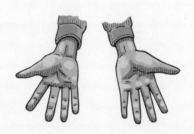

I ordered a **CHICKEN** and an **EGG** online.

I'll let you know which comes first.

A termite walks into a
BAR and asks,

"Is the bar tender here?"

Why did the octopus beat
the shark in a fight?

Because it was well armed.

What did **DADDY** spider say to baby spider?

You spend too much time on the **WEB.**

What do you call a group
of **KILLER WHALES**
playing instruments?

An orca-stra.

We might be going
SNORKELING
this weekend,

but I'm not holding my breath.

Why are **SKELETONS**
so calm?

Because nothing gets under their skin.

Why did the **BUNNY** go to the hospital?

*Because he needed a **HOP**eration.*

Why aren't
KOALAS bears?

They don't meet the koalafications.

Want to hear a **JOKE** about cats?

Just kitten!

I wanted to buy a pair of **CAMOUFLAGE** pants,

but I couldn't find them anywhere!

Why was the **CAT** asked to leave the **COMPUTER** store?

He wouldn't stop playing with the mouse.

What did the **KANGAROO** say when her baby was kidnapped?

"Someone help me catch that pickpocket!"

Why don't **BANKS** allow kangaroos to open accounts?

Because their checks always bounce.

How do you play leapfrog with a **PORCUPINE**?

Very carefully.

Why do **OCEANS** never go out of style?

They're always current.

One day I was in the park wondering why Frisbees get **BIGGER** . . .

and then it hit me.

Which letter has **THE MOST** water in it?

The *.*

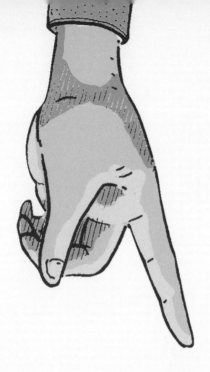

Have you heard the joke about the GIANT?

Never mind; it's over your head.

What did the angry **HEDGEHOG** say to its enemy?

"I'm going to quill you."

What did the **FISH** say when he swam into a wall?

"Dam."

What do you call a
BEE with a
QUIET buzz?

A mumblebee.

What if **CATS** have been trying to tell us they're in pain this entire time?

"Me ow?"

The credit card company sent me another **CAMOUFLAGED** bull!

*It's those **HIDDEN CHARGES** that you really have to watch out for.*

Why didn't the **DINOSAUR** cross the road?

Because roads weren't invented yet.

What do you call a bear with **NO EARS?**

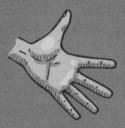

B.

What do you call a snake that's 3.14 meters long?

A pi-thon.

What's more impressive than a **TALKING DOG**?

A spelling bee.

Why do you have to be careful when it's raining cats and dogs?

You might step in a poodle!

Did you hear about the huge **SALE** on canoes?

It's quite the oar deal.

Where do animals go when they lose their **TAILS**?

To the retail store.

A lumberjack went into a magic forest and started to swing at a tree. It shouted, "Wait! I'm a **TALKING TREE!**"

The lumberjack replied, *"And you will dialogue!"*

I can cut **WOOD** just by looking at it. It's true!

I saw it with my own eyes!

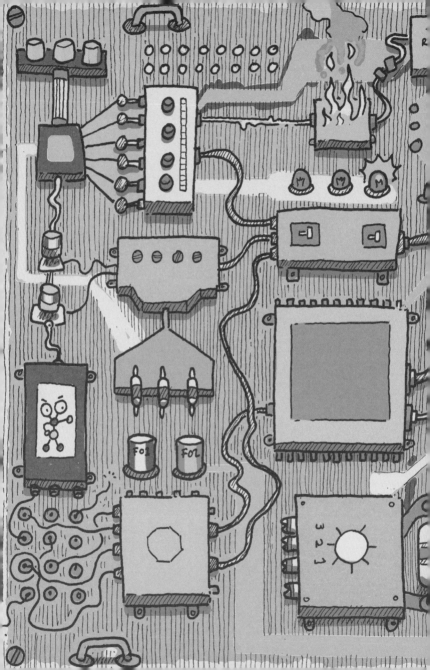

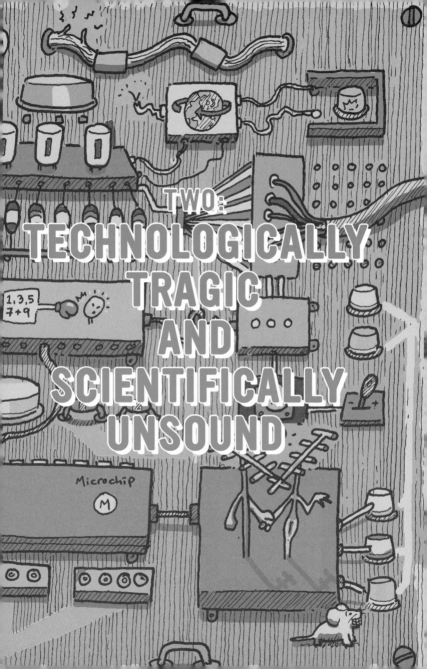

I gave all my dead batteries away . . .

free of charge.

To whoever stole my Microsoft **OFFICE** subscription:

I will find you. You have my Word.

I got an email that said:
"At Google Earth,
we can read maps
BACKWARD!"

But I trashed it, because that's just spam.

How do you drown
a **HIPSTER?**

In the mainstream.

DAUGHTER:
"What time is it?"

DAD: *"I don't know, it keeps changing!"*

DAD: "I think **FORTNITE** is a bad name for a video game."

DAUGHTER: "What? Why?!"

DAD: "I don't know, it's just two week."

What did the old lamp say to its new **LIGHT BULB**?

You've got a bright future, kid.

What do prisoners use to call each other?

Cell phones.

You know what we'd call it if prisoners could take their own mugshots?

Cellfies!

DAUGHTER:
"Can I watch the TV?"

DAD: *"Yes, but don't turn it on."*

What happened when the
TWO ANTENNAS
got married?

Well, the ceremony was kind of boring,
but the reception was great!

If you see a **ROBBERY**
at an Apple store,

does that make you an iWitness?

There's a thin line between a **NUMERATOR** and

a **DENOMINATOR**,

and only a fraction of people can understand that.

Geology rocks,

but geography is really where it's at.

Don't trust atoms.

They make up everything!

What did the molecule say to the **SUSPICIOUS** molecule?

"I've got my ion you."

Why should you wear **GLASSES** during math class?

They say it improves division.

PARALLEL lines have so much in common.

It's really too bad they'll never meet.

I was going to tell a
TIME TRAVEL joke,

but you didn't like it.

Did you hear about
that ATM who was
ADDICTED to money?

He suffered from withdrawals.

The rotation of the earth

really makes my day.

You heard of that new band **1023MB**?

They're good but they haven't got a gig yet.

Why did the **ASTRONAUT** move to the suburbs?

He needed more space.

My friends keep telling me I'm addicted to **BRAKE FLUID,**

but I can stop whenever I want.

What did the **MOUSE** say to the camera?

"Cheese!"

What do you get when you **CROSS** Microsoft Word with Dracula?

A word count.

I was at a yard sale the other day, and the guy was asking $50 for a TV. The **VOLUME** controls weren't working,

but at that price, I couldn't turn it down.

What is the **BEST TOOL** to make a car move?

A screwdriver.

I got in a fight with 1, 3, 5, 7, and 9.

The odds were against me.

The circle is the most **RIDICULOUS** shape in the world.

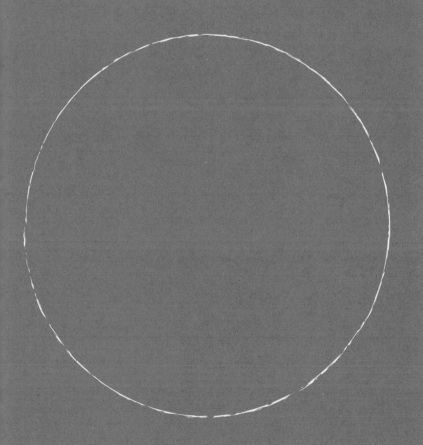

There's absolutely no point to it.

Scientists got **BORED** watching the earth turn,

1

so after 24 hours they called it a day.

Do you know what they call **BIGFOOT** in Europe?

Bigmeter.

How do **MICROSCOPIC ORGANISMS** call each other?

On microphones.

THREE:
FUNNY
FOODSTUFFS

Hey, have you ever tried to **EAT** a clock?

It's very time consuming.

SERVER: "Sorry about your **WAIT!**"

DAD: "Are you calling me fat?!"

What do you call a **NOSY** pepper?

Jalapeño business!

Two guys walk into a bar.

The third one ducks.

I had a nightmare that I drowned in an ocean of **ORANGE SODA,**

but thankfully, it was just a Fanta sea.

I hit my son in the head
with a Diet Coke today,
but he's **OKAY**.

It was just a soft drink.

HOSTESS: **"Did you have reservations?"**

DAD: *"Nope, I'm 100 percent confident that I want to eat here."*

What do you call a **LONELY** cheese?

Provolone.

Did you hear about
the restaurant on the **MOON**?

Great food, no atmosphere.

What did the **DADDY TOMATO** say to the **BABY TOMATO?**

"Catch up!"

Why did the girl smear peanut butter on the road?

To go with the traffic jam.

I'm on a seafood diet . . .

I see food and I eat it.

A guy walked into a bar . . .

and was disqualified from the limbo contest.

My **WIFE** is on a tropical foods diet, and the house is **FULL OF THE STUFF!**

It's enough to make a mango crazy.

A STEAK PUN

is a rare medium well done.

A slice of apple pie is $2.50 in Jamaica and $3.00 in the Bahamas.

These are the pie rates of the Caribbean.

JUSTICE is a dish best served cold.

If it were served warm,
it would be justwater.

What does a zombie
vegetarian eat?

GRAAAAIIIIIINNNSS.

Why did the can crusher decide to **QUIT** his job?

Because it was soda-pressing.

What do you call **CHEESE** that doesn't belong to you?

Nacho cheese.

I hate jokes about
GERMAN SAUSAGES.

They're the wurst.

What do you call a
fake **NOODLE**?

An impasta.

Why did the **COFFEE** file a police report?

It got mugged.

CASHIER: "Would you like the milk in a bag, sir?"

DAD: "No thank you, just leave it in the carton!"

What did the **BABY** corn say to the **MOM** corn?

"Where's popcorn?"

Where can I go to learn
HOW TO MAKE
ice cream?

Sundae school.

Did you hear about
the guy who invented
LIFESAVERS?

They say he made a mint.

I've been telling
everyone about the
benefits of eating
DRIED GRAPES.

I'm all about raisin awareness!

What did the **GRAPE** do when he got stepped on?

He let out a little wine.

What would an action movie about **PASTA** be called?

Mission Im-pasta-ble.

Want to hear a joke about **PIZZA**?

Never mind, it's too cheesy.

What do you call a bear with NO TEETH?

A gummy bear.

When is **CHICKEN SOUP** not good for your health?

If you're the chicken!

WAITER: "Do you wanna box for your **LEFTOVERS?**"

DAD: *"No, but I'll wrestle you for them!"*

Some guy just hit me in the face with a **CHEESE WHEEL**.

How dairy.

I was thinking of going on an all-almond diet.

But that's just nuts!

My wife and I were arguing as to who gets to use the **MICROWAVE** first.

Then things started to get heated.

Did you hear the joke about the **BUTTER?**

I'd better not tell you; it might spread.

I thought about becoming **VEGAN** . . .

until I realized it would be a big

missed steak.

SERVER: "And how did you find your steak this evening?"

CUSTOMER: *"Oh, it was easy; I just looked under the parsley."*

What did
AUNT JEMIMA
say when she ran out
of **PANCAKES**?

"How waffle."

If **TWO VEGANS** get in an argument,

is it still considered a beef?

"You have a 'dad bod!'"

DAD: *"I like to think of it more as a father figure."*

It's **HARD TO SAY**
what my wife
does for a living.

She sells seashells by the seashore.

What do you call a HIPPIE'S wife?

Mississippi.

I swapped our bed for a **TRAMPOLINE**.

My wife hit the roof.

DAD: "Knock knock!"

DAUGHTER: "Who's there?"

DAD: "Control freak."

DAUGHTER: "Con—"

DAD: "Okay, now you say 'Control freak who?'"

Have we ever told you kids about OUR WEDDING?

It was so beautiful that even the cake was in tiers.

My wife says I'm **INDECISIVE**, but I don't think I am!

Unless you think I should be?

Today, my son asked me, "Can I have a **BOOKMARK?**" and I burst into tears.

Eleven years old, and he still doesn't know my name is Brian.

DAD: "Did you hear the one about the bed?"

SON: "No!"

DAD: "That's because it hasn't been made yet."

SON: "Where are my SUNGLASSES?"

DAD: "I don't know . . . where are my dad glasses?"

I'd like to thank
SIDEWALKS everywhere

for keeping my kids off the streets!

My daughter is **TERRIFIED** of elevators,

so we're going to start **taking steps** *to avoid them.*

DAUGHTER: **"Dad, can you put MY SHOES on?"**

DAD: *"I can try, but I don't think they'll fit me."*

After dinner my wife asked me if I could **CLEAR** the table.

I needed to get a running start, but I made it.

SON: **"I'll call you later!"**

DAD: *"Don't call me later. Call me Dad."*

SON: "Dad, why are you back early?"

DAD: "My boss told me to have a good day, so I came home!"

Kids, you must always
remember the three
**UNWRITTEN RULES
OF LIFE.**

1._____

2._____

3._____

My wife told me to stop imitating a flamingo.

So I had to put my foot down.

SON: "Dad, did you get a haircut?"

DAD: "No, I got them all cut!"

I thought at least a couple of **MY PUNS** would make you laugh,

but no pun in 10 did.

My children accuse me of liking **COURTROOM PUNS** too much.

I'm guilty as charged.

MOM: **"How do I look?"**

DAD: *"With your eyes."*

I couldn't decide how much lettuce to buy, but **MY WIFE HELPED ME** think through it.

Two heads are better than one.

My wife said I should try to do **LUNGES** to stay in shape.

That would be a big step forward for me.

If a child **REFUSES TO SLEEP** during naptime,

are they guilty of resisting a rest?

My daughter shrieked, "Daaaaaad, **YOU HAVEN'T LISTENED** to a single word I've said, have you!?"

I thought that a strange way to start a conversation with me . . .

DAUGHTER: "Dad, why are you staring at the **ORANGE JUICE** container?"

DAD: *"It said concentrate!"*

My wife is really mad
that I have **NO SENSE
OF DIRECTION**.

 So I packed up my stuff and right.

SON: **"Wait up, Dad, I have something in my shoe!"**

DAD: *"I'm pretty sure it's a foot."*

My kids were very upset when our bunnies ESCAPED.

They're too young to deal with hare loss.

How does **DARTH VADER** like his toast?

On the dark side.

I never wanted to believe that my dad was **STEALING** from his job as a road worker.

But when I got home,
all the signs were there.

WIFE: "Do you think our kids are spoiled?"

HUSBAND: "No, I think most kids smell like that."

DAD: "Is there a **HOLE** in your shoe?"

SON: "No . . ."

DAD: "Well, then how'd you get your foot in it?"

When should you bring **YOUR FATHER** to class?

When you have a pop quiz.

I asked my wife what she wanted for Christmas. She said, "**NOTHING** would make me happier than a diamond necklace!"

So I gave her nothing.

DAD: "What do you want for dinner?"

SON: "I feel like SPAGHETTI."

DAD: "That's funny, you don't look like spaghetti . . ."

DAUGHTER: **"Dad, can you please call me a TAXI?"**

DAD: *"Sure. You're a taxi."*

DAD: "Make sure you put on your **HELMET** before using the computer!"

SON: "Why . . .?"

DAD: *"It might crash!"*

After my wife had given birth to our baby, the nurse asked me, "Do you have a name yet?" I said, "Yes. Steve." She said, "Awww!
THAT'S A LOVELY NAME!"

"Thanks," I said. "But what do you think we should call the baby?"

I told my son I was named **AFTER THOMAS JEFFERSON**. He said, "But Dad, your name is **BRIAN**."

I said, "I know, but I was named AFTER Thomas Jefferson."

DAUGHTER: "Nothing rhymes with orange."

DAD: "No it doesn't."

How do people **LOSE** their kids in a mall?

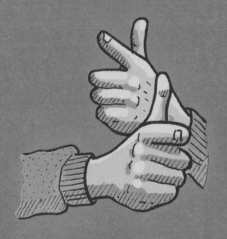

Seriously, any tips are welcome.

SON: "Hey Dad,
I'm taking a shower."

DAD: "Okay, just make sure to bring it back."

An invisible woman MARRIES an invisible man.

The kids were nothing to look at either.

My wife tripped and dropped the basket of clothes she had **JUST IRONED**.

I watched it all unfold.

FIVE:
THE ARTS AND THE
COMEDIC ARTIST

Did you hear about the actor who **FELL** through the floorboards?

He was just going through a stage.

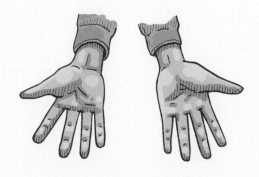

SON: "Which **HAND** do you write with?"

DAD: *"Gosh, neither. I write with a pen!"*

Why didn't the vampire attack **TAYLOR SWIFT?**

She had "Bad Blood."

My son bought me a **REALLY CHEAP** dictionary for my birthday.

I couldn't find the words to thank him.

DAD: "Can I have a play by Shakespeare?"

BOOKSTORE CLERK: "Of course, sir! Which one were you looking for?"

DAD: "William."

Accordion to a recent survey,

inserting musical instruments into sentences goes largely unnoticed.

I
dig,
you
dig,
she
digs,
he
digs,
we
dig,
they
dig.

It's not a very long poem,
but it is deep.

How do you find
WILL SMITH
in the snow?

Look for the fresh prints!

My daughter asked me to stop singing
"I'M A BELIEVER" and
I thought she was joking!

But then I saw her face . . .

How much does a
HIPSTER weigh?

An Instagram.

I'm reading a book on the history of **GLUE**.

I can't seem to put it down!

Why were the **DARK AGES** so dark?

Too many knights.

The biggest knight at
KING ARTHUR's
round table was
Sir Cumference.

He acquired his size from too much pi.

Want to hear a joke about **PAPER**?

Never mind; it's tearable.

Have you ever heard of a music group called CELLOPHANE?

They mostly wrap.

What is Whitney Houston's favorite type of **COORDINATION**?

HAND EEEEEEEEEEEYEEEEEEEEEE!

UP NEXT: How to sound good in a band.

Stay tuned!

I used to be addicted to the **HOKEY POKEY**.

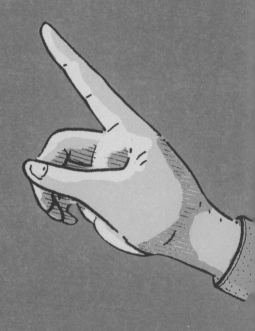

But then I turned myself around.

How do you make a
BANDSTAND?

Take away their chairs.

What kind of **MUSIC** do
they play at a playground?

Swing.

Why did the **BEATLES** break up?

They started to bug each other.

What kind of MUSIC
do balloons hate?

Pop.

Why was the artist arrested for graffiti?

They had to draw the line somewhere.

What kind of music do **WINDMILLS** like?

I hear they're big metal fans . . .

Why are **PRISONERS** not good musicians?

Because they're always behind a few bars and can't find the key.

It's been years since I've done the **HOKEY POKEY**.

I forget what it's all about.

What did
DJ ALLERGIES
say to the nose?

"Drop it like it's snot."

What kind of music do **MUMMIES** listen to?

Wrap music.

What **ROCK GROUP** has four men that don't sing?

Mount Rushmore.

NURSE: **"Do you know your BLOOD TYPE?"**

DAD: *"Sure, it's the red one."*

I was addicted to **SOAP** when I was your age,

but I've been clean for thirty years.

[An **AMBULANCE** flies by with its sirens blaring.]

DAD: *"They won't sell much ice cream going that fast!"*

Why did the barber win the race?

He knew a shortcut.

You know, people say they pick their nose,

but I feel like I was just born with mine.

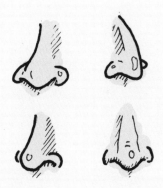

Why can't a nose grow to be **TWELVE INCHES** long?

Because then it would be a foot!

I have **KLEPTOMANIA**.

Sometimes when it gets really bad, I take something for it.

I keep trying
to **LOSE** weight,

but it keeps finding me.

I've just been diagnosed with **COLOR BLINDNESS**.

I know, it really came out of the purple!

What do you call someone with **NO** body and **NO** nose?

Nobody knows.

How do you make a **KLEENEX** dance?

Put a little boogie in it!

I used to hate facial hair,

but now it's growing on me.

This **GRAVEYARD**
looks overcrowded.

People must be dying to get in there.

What time did the man go to the dentist?

Tooth hurt-y.

"Doctor, I've broken my arm in several places."

DOCTOR: *"Well, don't go to those places."*

Why do optimists have to wear sunglasses?

Because they always look at the bright side!

I can't believe **VIRUSES** and **BACTERIA** just enter my body without permission.

That makes me sick . . .

You know what makes me SMILE?

Face muscles.

With **GREAT REFLEXES** . . .

comes great response ability.

I had the weirdest dream last night; I dreamt I was a **MUFFLER**.

I woke up exhausted.

I have an intense fear of **SPEED BUMPS,**

but I'm slowly getting over it.

Just so everybody's clear,

I'm going to put my glasses on.

A man tried to sell me a COFFIN today.

I told him that's the last thing I need.

My earliest childhood memory is getting my first pair of **GLASSES**.

Life before that was a blur.

A **TOILET** was stolen from the police station.

Police report they have nothing to go on.

My **RECLINER** and I

go way back.

I don't **TRUST** stairs.

They're always up to something.

If you **REARRANGE** the letters of "mailman,"

they get really mad.

I'm only familiar with
25 LETTERS in the
English language.

I don't know why.

Why couldn't the bike stand up by itself?

It was two tired.

I used to work in a shoe **RECYCLING** shop.

It was sole destroying.

Why wasn't the woman happy with the **VELCRO** she bought?

It was a total ripoff.

Whatever happened to the guy **WHO INVENTED** the knock-knock joke?

I heard he won the no-bell prize!

Did you hear about the **NEW STORE** that just opened?

It's called Moderation, and they have every-
thing there!

What kind of **SHOES** do thieves wear?

Sneakers.

I went to the
CORNER SHOP today.

I bought four corners.

Why don't skeletons go TRICK-OR-TREATING?

Because they don't have any body to go with.

I used to have a job at a CALENDAR factory,

but I got fired because I took a couple of days off.

I don't play **SOCCER** because I enjoy the sport.

I'm just doing it for kicks.

What word starts with "E" and ends with "E" and only has one LETTER in it?

Envelope.

,

I'll never date
another **APOSTROPHE**.

The last one was too possessive.

When is a **DOOR**
not a door?

When it's ajar.

Why was the PICTURE sent to jail?

It was framed.

Want to hear a joke about CONSTRUCTION?

Never mind—I'm still working on it.

What's the advantage of living in Switzerland?

Well, the flag is a big plus.

Did you hear about the
new **BROOM** on
the market?

It's sweeping the nation.

I'm giving my chimney away for free.

You could say it's on the house.

Where do snowmen and **SNOWWOMEN** go to dance?

The snow ball.

What kind of school does **SHERLOCK HOLMES** attend?

Elementary, my dear Watson.

Why was the
BASKETBALL COURT
all wet?

People kept dribbling all over it.

How did the giant know that Jack was coming?

She heard Jack and the beans talk.

What did the rope say when it got **TANGLED**?

"Oh no, knot again!"

How can you get four suits for just **ONE DOLLAR?**

Buy a deck of cards.

What made the newspaper **BLUSH?**

It saw the comic strip.

Why are **GHOSTS** great **CHEERLEADERS?**

Because they have a lot of spirit.

Did you hear about the guy who **STOLE A CALENDAR?**

He got 12 months.

Have you read the
ARTICLE ABOUT CLOCKS?

If not, it's about time.

I didn't play well in my
BASKETBALL GAME
yesterday.

I really dropped the ball.

Why shouldn't you feed
TEDDY BEARS?

They're already stuffed.

I'm going to **REWRITE** history.

HISTORY.

What's blue and smells like RED PAINT?

Blue paint.

What did the janitor say when he **JUMPED OUT** of the closet?

Supplies!

How do **BILLBOARDS** talk?

In sign language.

What's blue and
NOT VERY HEAVY?

Light blue.

Someone said they liked
MY NAME.

I said, "Thanks! I got it for my birthday!"

I'm very worried for
THE CALENDAR.

Its days are numbered!

Have you ever heard the
joke about the **LETTER**
without a **STAMP**?

Eh, you wouldn't get it.

Why are **TENNIS PLAYERS** bad in relationships?

Because love means nothing to them.

My friend keeps saying, "**CHEER UP!** It could be worse: you could be stuck underground in a **HOLE FULL OF WATER**."

I know he means well.

I think I want to quit my job and **CLEAN MIRRORS** for a living instead.

It's just something I can see myself doing.

How are **PLATEAUS** similar to imitation?

They're both the highest forms of flattery.

HARRY POTTER can't tell the difference between his cooking pot and his best friend.

They're both cauldron.

I finally bought the **THESAURUS** that I've always wanted. When I opened it, all the pages were **BLANK**.

I have no words to describe how angry I am.

QUEUE is just one letter followed by four **SILENT LETTERS.**

They must be waiting for their turn.

Would anyone be interested in being **MY COMPANION?**

Asking for a friend.

What has **FOUR LETTERS,** sometimes has nine,

and never has five . . .

Statistically **6 OUT OF 7 DWARVES** aren't happy.

I went into the library and asked if they had any books on the **TITANIC**. "Yes, quite a few," the librarian said.

"Sorry to hear that!" I said. "They'll all be ruined by now!"

My friend asked me if I could name two different structures that hold water.

I said, "Well, dam . . ."

I was told not to **STEAL** the kitchen utensils.

But it's a whisk I'm willing to take.

Why are there no **KNOCK-KNOCK** jokes about America?

Because freedom rings.

ACKNOWLEDGMENTS

THANK YOU to the dads everywhere who endure whiny children, constant demands, and pleas for rides to the mall while still managing to crack a bad joke through it all.

Thank you to my parents, Hudson and Suzana, who made laughter and corny jokes a way of life and who still won't stop telling that awful one about the tomato crossing the street.

Thank you to Ariel Vogel and Sarah Quagliariello, whose detailed and diligent editorial work made this book what it is.

Thank you to Maria Ribas at Stonesong for her ceaseless belief and boundless enthusiasm for this project (and for contributing a few bad jokes herself).

An extra big thank you to Becca Hunt, the best editor a dad joke book could have. Thank you for understanding this project, shaping it to be infinitely better, and making the whole process so ridiculously fun.

And thank you to the entire team at Chronicle Books, whose talent and thoughtfulness has made this book much more than the sum of its jokes.